AXIOMS FOR WORK/LIFE

Mirelle Vraimont

AXIOMS FOR WORK/LIFE

Manufactured in the United States of America by:

www.lulu.com

ISBN: 978-0-6151-3699-8

DEDICATION

To my mother:

M. A. Briggs, an elegant and knowledgeable Southern lady!

For all my endeavors, you have offered encouragement, guidance, and love. You brought the wisdom of Grandma Amanda, which she so aptly instilled in you during her short time on this earth. I thank you for all that you brought and for sharing, caring, giving and most of all, for loving me!

m.v.

FOREWORD

What is said to you as you journey through life will stay with you forever. If it is good, it will influence your life for the better. If it is negative, it will provide a constant source of sadness.

We thrive on things that lift us up and inspire us! Just think of the radiant smiles of a child when he is paid a compliment; if you are given a promotion at your job for good work, how elated you are!

Remember always that words are like swords. If sheathed and properly used, they are wonderful protection. If unsheathed and improperly used, they can do considerable harm.

These axioms have come your way at different times, "clothed in different clothing." Future volumes will explore more "saws" from this country and around the world. Let me hear from you!

Mirelle Vraimont
www.dseyafanel@hotmail.com

**Thoughts float like snowflakes
to create an intellectual
blizzard!**

**Don't make a promise you
can't keep!**

Great intellectual ideas are
spun by the intermingling
of ordinary minds.

**A rose is the headdress of a
thorn!**

Revolving doors teach a valuable lesson: If you don't step out on your own, you have no choice but to continue going in circles.

If getting your new promotion is like "taking candy from a baby", evaluate the worth of the promotion.

Every sunrise is a new opportunity to succeed.

**What one constantly thinks
will become a reality.**

A pearl is an abnormal
"happening," but beautiful
just the same!

How are words like knives?
Once they cut you, the
scar remains!

What you take away from the table depends largely upon what you bring to the table.

**If you are always prepared,
when the fire springs forth,
you'll have water.**

If you allow your mind to become static, your ability to think will be compromised.

**Do not ignore illiteracy; it
can inhibit the power
to think!**

Fear paralyzes!

**Constructive criticism is a
valuable tool; criticism for
the sake of criticism is cruel!**

If life was not supposed to
have ups and downs, there
would be no hills and valleys.

Kindness is innate!

Duplicity is not the cousin of integrity.

**Enterprising people exhibit
initiative!**

Wealth is the result of serious accounting!

Organization doesn't just
happen; it's the product of a
structured mind.

If you decide to climb the proverbial ladder, rid yourself of hangers on.

**Impetuosity breeds
disappointment.**

When laughter enters the
room, sadness makes a
hasty exit.

There will always be
occasions where silence is
mandatory.

**Good manners are the result
of constant practice.**

An insincere compliment
is worse than no
compliment at all.

**The mask of hypocrisy is
often transparent.**

Hypothetical statements should always be examined.

**Transient perfection should
be admired.**

**Incentives are the motivators
of action!**

**True friendship is not
diminished by truth!**

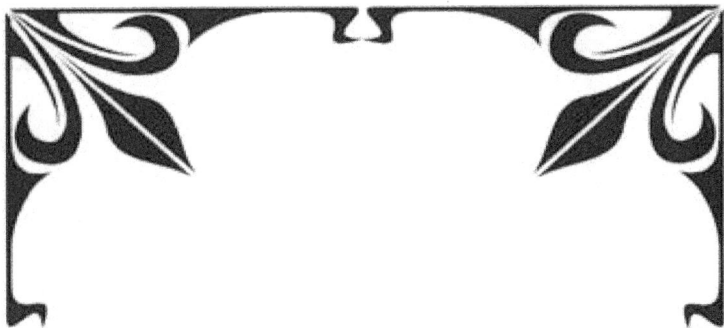

**Resolute people seldom follow
irresponsible paths.**

**Mediocrity does not interest
the illustrious mind.**

**The creative mind shows you
what you cannot see!**

Health is priceless!

**A poem can paint a picture
in the dark!**

Compliance is a necessary implement of subordination.

Inconsistency spawns indecision.

**A half-hearted effort is
uninspiring.**

The warmth of a smile symbolizes the luminescence of the heart.

Twinkling stars remind us of our diminution in the universe.

Grains of sand on a beach,
though temporarily repressed,
are refreshed with the tide!

If you find yourself in a crisis, be decisive!

When a task requires exertion, think only of the strength you'll build; not the attendant fatigue.

**Moderation is the balancer
for both extravagance
and miserliness!**

Experiment with life; you
never know what the outcome
will be.

An expert has an edge; he
knows his "files."

If others walk on you, demonstrate your resilience!

To gloat over another's
misfortune, portends your
own adversity.

Unless you examine the facts carefully, you will be unable to dispute the outcome!

**An erudite professor is not
a guarantee of a
well-taught class!**

Action is the precursor of accomplishment.

**Straightforward answers
minimize mistakes!**

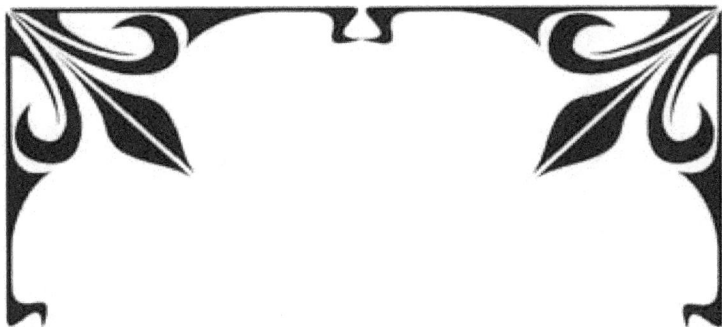

**Digression is the author
of puzzlement.**

**Influence is a tool of
the powerful!**

When friends are disloyal, you are reminded that they can be "wolves in sheep's clothing."

New friends are keepsakes;
old friends are treasures.

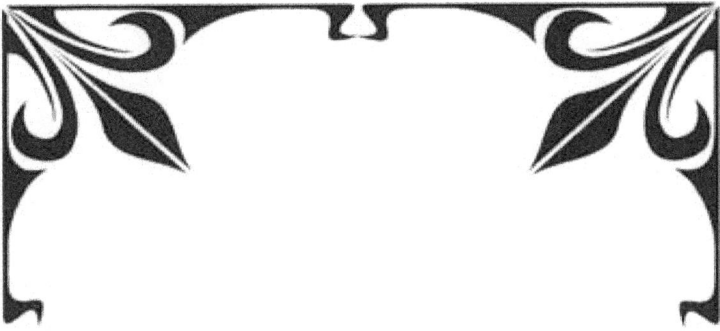

Knowing where you are going allows you to avoid misplacing your energies.

**The likelihood of failure
is ever present: Defeat
it with achievement!**

A suitcase is like a dishwasher;
it holds the things you
need to wash.

Trees, if unable to grow straight
up, will grow sideways until
they find their energy source
(the sun). Grow in any
direction until you find
your energy source!

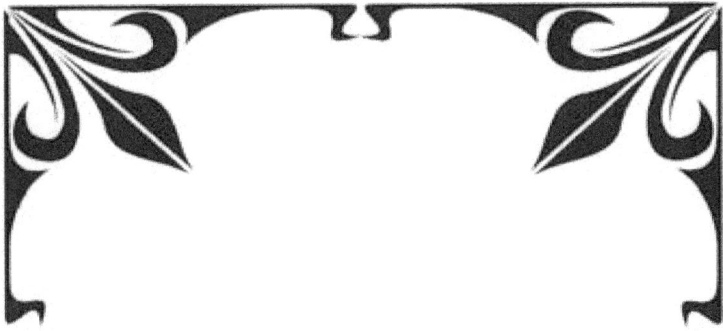

**Starlight gives flight to
imagination!**

If you are dissatisfied with everything, you will dissatisfy everyone.

Sanction of a plan is not
always authorization to
proceed.

**What fits a king is not always
fit for a king.**

**When precision is needed,
a makeshift plan won't do!**

**Identify your friends before
your enemies arrive!**

Apathy is not an exemplary quality!

How is a bunch of flowers like
a bunch of grapes? Refreshing,
fragrant, and colorful!

Corruption precedes ultimate decline!

**To reach the heights of life,
one must experience
the depths!**

**Resting on your laurels is
a waste of precious time!**

Ignorance of etiquette can
stymie an otherwise
perfect encounter.

A full moon is a reminder
that illumination can come
from many sources.

The Titanic was a colossal example of natural vulnerability.

The harbor is a perfect shelter
for disabled vessels; where
should disabled thinkers go?

If you are a perfectionist
who desires pinpoint
exactitude, get a pin
cushion.

If you ever expect to reach
the pinnacle, you must
continue the climb.

If you're always seeking the ultimate rush, you'll miss life's daily satisfactions!

Reaching for the stars can
be a destabilizing
experience.

If you don't think salmon
are tenacious, try
swimming upstream!

Create your own legacy!

Peace will not be delivered
on the wings of a dove.
It must be avidly sought.

Chiggers (tiny red bugs)
are like enemies.
They burrow deeply
and cause discomfort.

**In politics, the sensible choice
is not always the logical
choice!**

**Ace your opponents to
avoid love!**

**Disgrace *to* you can only
come *from* you!**

Spending money is like dieting:

Spending money: If you write down what you spend, you won't be surprised when your pockets are empty.

Dieting: If you write down what you eat, you won't be surprised by the extra pounds.

Power is transient!

Need is a powerful motivator.

Reading another person's eyes
is a great barometer as to
how your comments
are being received.

Attitude is everything!

Showing compassion for
another's difficulties
earns gratefulness you
can't measure!

Achievement, endurance, and
persistence are like rain, snow,
and hail: Parts of a
similar process!

Mirelle Vraimont is an internationally renowned concert artist who has traveled to more than fifteen different countries in the pursuit of excellence in her craft and whose life experiences have bordered on everything from the tragic to the hilarious; from shocking misfortune to extreme good fortune; from anguish to contentment.

In addition to her international travels, she is a published poet, philosopher, author; teacher, parent, publisher, and patent holder. She has more than 35 years experience in the creative arts and education.

Each individual's life experiences, while different and personal, are often mirrored in the life experiences of others. Our mothers, grandmothers, aunts, great-aunts, coaches, teachers, etc., all gave us statements to provide a series of life's lessons according to their experiences. Mirelle wrote this book with the hope that you will see yourself and some of those around you in these pages and that these reminders will continue to provide life's lessons!